From the Card

Dear Friends,

I want to commend
know from talking t
these small prayer books have been. Not only have the people using them found them a valuable aid to deepening their life of prayer but they have also helped the Diocesan process of pastoral and spiritual renewal be rooted in prayer. I am sure that this prayer from so many in the Diocese has been important to the success of the renewal programme.

So keep on finding out what God is saying to you each day in the Scriptures, not only in Season V but beyond.

Be assured of my part in this "community of prayer".

With every blessing

+Cormac

Archbishop of Westminster

Building the Kingdom

Many years ago the priest who taught me about prayer said that I should never talk about private prayer. For the Christian, prayer is never private but some prayer can be – indeed should be – personal.

These meditation booklets have been written to help your personal prayer in the knowledge that your personal prayer will be part of that great stream of prayer that goes up to Heaven from this Diocese. This is especially pertinent in Season V when we are focused on how to live the values of the Gospel. You are a vital part of a team which is helping the Diocese realise the truth that God is waiting to give us new blessings.

The experience of working as a team is one of the rich blessings of the *At Your Word, Lord* Renewal Programme. We have achieved so much because we have worked together. People in parishes, employees of the Diocese and various church agencies as well as colleagues around the country and beyond have been our supporters, our collaborators.

Collaboration works and everyone has a role to play. Never forget that those who pray are players too!

God bless you

Stuart Wilson

Fr. Stuart Wilson
Director

Introduction

This Autumn sees the Diocese of Westminster enter its fifth and last Season of *At Your Word, Lord*. This meditation booklet is designed to help the reader to reflect on our call to *Recreate the Face of the Earth – Build the Kingdom of God* by living the values that Christ teaches in the Gospels. Prayer and the experience of sharing faith in small groups have made a great impact on many people's lives, and on parish communities and so we invite you to pray daily with these meditations.

The style of this booklet remains similar to that of previous Seasons. Each day has a short text from Scripture, which is usually drawn from the Mass readings of that day. It is God's own Word to us, and we use it to make it a conversation with God. The brief daily reflection may help to direct thoughts or increase our understanding of the passage. The closing prayer may help to focus on a priority for the day.

We suggest that, as far as possible, you choose a regular time each day to use this booklet. Remind yourself as you begin that this is a special time just for you to spend with God. Start by thanking God for this moment of prayer and ask Him to help you to pray. Read through the Scripture passage, pause and then re-read it very slowly. See if the reflection helps to concentrate your thoughts. Stop to reflect and absorb any phrase or word that seems to stand out and speak to you. Determine to carry that word or phrase with you throughout the day. Do not allow your prayer to be rushed – if you choose to pray for ten or fifteen minutes try to see that period of time to the end – new thoughts may arrive even though you might feel that you have read and absorbed the text. You might even find it helpful to write the phrase or word on a piece of paper as a reminder, to keep the sense of prayer with you between your times of meditation. This booklet is small enough to carry in a pocket or bag.

May this time in prayer increase the sense of the presence of God in your life, influencing all that you are doing, and being a part of the decisions and choices of each day.

Preparing the Way for Season V – Starting Out

1 Thessalonians 1:2-3

We always mention you in our prayers and thank God for you all, and constantly remember before God our Father how you have shown your faith in action, worked for love and persevered through hope, in our Lord Jesus Christ.

These words come from the Second Reading of Mass on the opening day of Season V. It might just remind me of the wider vision of my faith and what I am trying to do through meditation. This is my starting place for a season of meditation. Paul puts together in just a few words my life of faith, as it should be: a combination of works, faith, love and hope. They all go together and they weave themselves into every aspect of my life, whether at work or college, at home, in my social life with friends and when I come to pray. This is to be my life. Where I discover places where I have shut God out, or pretend that He does not belong – this is exactly the place where I must learn to invite Him in. He must be part of everything that I do and say, the decisions that I make, in my asking and thanksgiving. By these times of meditation during the next six weeks, I will try to live in the presence of God each day – all day.

Father, guide my thoughts, my words and my actions, so that everything that I do may be pleasing to you and that I may recognise your presence in every part of my life.

Week One
Loving the Poor

The Gospel speaks clearly and often about the need for compassion for, and solidarity with, the poor. If we are to follow Jesus, we too must be compassionate towards the poor, whether their poverty is material or spiritual. Despite many efforts to alleviate material poverty in our world, the gap between rich and poor, be they individuals or nations, is expanding. We are all challenged to bring poverty to an end; to make poverty history.

Sunday: Luke 14:13-14
(29th Sunday of the Year)

No; when you have a party, invite the poor, the crippled, the lame, the blind; that they cannot pay you back means that you are fortunate, because repayment will be made to you when the virtuous rise again.

Literally speaking, there would be few people who could meet this challenge and invite the poor, crippled, lame and blind into their homes. But there is a very practical and achievable call in these words: to be generous, and to be able to give without expecting return. In a world where we are encouraged to do things for ourselves, where "this is time for me" and we are told that it is good to pamper ourselves, it is all too easy to lose sight of generosity. The world's initial response to the Tsunami of December 2004 was a dramatic reminder that together we can make a difference and our generosity can change the world.

Jesus, help me to remember that, even in the smallest gestures of generosity, great things can be achieved.

Monday: Luke 12:19-21
(St Ignatius of Antioch)

"And I will say to my soul, Soul, you have plenty of good things laid by for many years to come; take things easy, eat, drink, have a good time." But God said to him, "Fool! This very night the demand will be made for your soul, and this hoard of yours, whose will it be then?" So it is when a man stores up treasure for himself in place of making himself rich in the sight of God.

Have I ever stopped to think how much I have? I probably do not need to worry where the next meal will come from. Shops and supermarkets provide me with endless choice. I have a roof over my head and, although there may be some things that I would still like to have, my home may already have many gadgets and time-saving electrical equipment. I can reasonably expect to travel on holiday and I have more than enough clothing and possessions. Instead of thinking about the things I do not have, I will begin to recognise all that I have and be grateful for it. The more difficult challenge comes if I ask myself how I use what I have? Does anyone else benefit from the possessions and the freedom that I have? Do I ever think of the needs of those around me?

> *Father, help me to be more aware of all that I have, and how I use it. May I be grateful for the good things of life, and may I grow in generosity to those who have not.*

Week One

Tuesday: Luke 6:20-21
(St Luke, Evangelist)

Then fixing his eyes on his disciples he said: "How happy are you who are poor: yours is the kingdom of God. Happy you who are hungry now: you shall be satisfied".

More than the other Gospel writers, Luke writes about the compassion of Jesus for the poor. He was 'moved' with compassion. When He saw the poverty of those around Him, it affected Him and He wanted to act with and for them. He even declares the poor to be 'holy' and proclaims that in their nothingness, in all their deprivation, it is they who have the Kingdom of God. Do I recognise holiness in the poor, or are they rather an embarrassment, an inconvenience – a reminder of my own vulnerability?

Father, may I value the holiness of the poor, recognising that I have the means and the resources to begin to change the deprivation of the world in which they live.

Wednesday: Luke 12:48
When a man has had a great deal given him, a great deal will be demanded of him; when a man has had a great deal given him on trust, even more will be expected of him.

Rather than allow myself to feel guilty, or overwhelmed, as I read this passage, I am invited to see the opportunity that it brings. I have so much: health, material possessions, friends. But all these blessings in my life are not just for me to enjoy for myself alone – they are there for a purpose, a means to an end. God Himself has entrusted these things to me, to be used wisely, so that these things may fulfil their potential through my stewardship. How awful it would be if on the last day Jesus were to stand at the gate of heaven and say "But look at all I gave you. Why did you not use it?"

Father, in recognising all that I have, may I use it for your greater service.

Thursday: 2 Corinthians 8:13-15

This does not mean that to give relief to others you ought to make things difficult for yourselves: it is a question of balancing what happens to be your surplus now against their present need, and one day they may have something to spare that will supply your own need. That is how we strike a balance: as Scripture says: The man who gathered much had none too much, the man who gathered little did not go short.

Paul tells us to give liberally whenever we are able, confident that, whenever we might be in need, we will receive in return. To use Paul's own word here, there is a careful 'balance' to be made. Prudence and just good common sense would tell us to save for retirement, to have something put aside ready 'for a rainy day'. But there is the call, too, to help others who are in need right now and to give from the surplus that we have. There is a test in faith here. If I am generous now, can I trust that God will provide for me when I am in need? But then, has God ever not provided for me?

Lord, teach me good stewardship so that I may know how to save and spend and where to balance the right priorities in my life.

Friday: Romans 7:18-19

The fact is, I know of nothing good living in me – living, that is, in my unspiritual self – for though the will to do what is good is in me, the performance is not, with the result that instead of doing the good things I want to do, I carry out the sinful thing I do not want.

Paul recognised that being true to faith in Christ is not easy and we often do not even seem to do the very things that we not only ought to do, but that we actually want to do. Our best intentions are frustrated because we cannot seem to be as good as we should be. But none of that disappointment deterred Paul from trying and persevering. Our best is not usually anywhere near perfection, but it is still valued by God. We know how wonderful it can be to see a small child learning to walk. There is no grace or elegance and within a few steps balance and coordination are lost and the child topples to the ground – but we know that determination and practice will gradually improve this child's efforts. God is just as charmed by our clumsy efforts, but will He find me just as determined as that child to succeed?

Father, despite my disappointments and failures, I am trying to do what is right and good. Give me a spirit of perseverance.

Saturday: 2 Corinthians 13:11

In the meantime, brothers, we wish you happiness; try to grow perfect; help one another. Be united; live in peace, and the God of love and peace will be with you.

We can draw some comfort from the fact that industrialised nations are at least talking about poverty in our world. Perhaps I cannot change the course of a nation's priorities single-handedly but there are times when I might be able to influence matters by supporting campaigns or lobbying Members of Parliament. I can also help at a local level and could make a firm commitment to an established charity or simply determine to help someone I know who is in need. I can make a difference.

Father, open my eyes to the needs of those around me and direct my efforts through even my small gestures of generosity.

Week Two
Loving the Earth

God created the earth out of love. How well do we love God's creation? Do we see ourselves as having arbitrary power to exploit it, or can we grow in our relationship with our planet, taking only what we need to sustain and nourish us? Now is a unique time for us to renew our values and to change insensitive attitudes and destructive actions that harm the earth.

Sunday: Genesis 1:31-2:1

(30th Sunday of the Year)

God saw all he had made, and indeed it was very good. Evening came and morning came: the sixth day. Thus heaven and earth were completed with all their array.

Week Two

Our knowledge of the universe continues to grow, as does our understanding of evolution. But we are only just beginning to grasp the immensity of God's creation and to measures its wonders. Our faith tells us that God created our world – and indeed it is good. He created it out of love and He asks us to share in that continuing work of creation through our stewardship. The idea that He created the world in seven days may be a fanciful story but it presents us with the fact that we exist, and the world has being, because God initiated His great plan – out of love.

Father, I thank you for the wonder of my being, for the immensity of the world that you have made, and for the mystery of your love in creation.

Monday: Mark: 4:26-29

'This is what the kingdom of God is like. A man throws seed on the land. Night and day, while he sleeps, when he is awake, the seed is sprouting and growing; how, he does not know. Of its own accord the land produces first the shoot, then the ear, then the full grain in the ear. And when the crop is ready, he loses no time: he starts to reap because the harvest has come'.

The miracle of creation is not just something to be seen at night in moon and stars, or marvelled at in the beauty of a mountain range or the immensity of the ocean. The same miracle of creation daily provides everything that we eat, the making of everything that we have, and use. Creation continues each day. its power and diversity increasingly entrusted into our hands. Will we harvest and renew, or just exploit, consume and extinguish?

Lord, guide us in the way we enjoy your gift of creation. May we sustain it and nurture it, and lose nothing of its beauty and diversity for the generations to come.

Tuesday: Psalm 117:24
This day was made by the Lord; we rejoice and are glad

The creation of each day is a gift from God to be savoured in joy and gratitude. The more we value the earth, the more we will work to save it. The sacrifice, hard work and risk-taking that are involved in preserving the earth flow from a growing relationship of love with God. It is in His creation that we live and move and have our being.

Father, may we value each day as a gift which brings both responsibilities and opportunities. May we care for your creation as we provide for our needs.

Wednesday: Romans 8:22
(SS Chad & Cedd)

From the beginning till now the entire creation, as we know, has been groaning in one great act of giving birth.

Our lifestyle can be either a blessing or a curse for the earth. We can choose life and protect our planet's resources by choosing a simpler lifestyle. Our individual and corporate economic decisions must increasingly consider their impact on future generations as well as on our own. Who would have thought it; but our faith might just be calling us to see the importance of a 'reducing, reusing, recycling' mentality!

Father, in the life choices that I make each day, may I think of the consequences of the lifestyle that I have. May my actions be a blessing, not a curse, for your creation.

Thursday: Psalm 24:1

To the Lord belong earth and all it holds, the world and all who live in it.

What we say that we 'own' is not really ours to use any way we want. Ultimately, all our property, possessions and talents are gifts from God for our responsible use and for the service of others. And what we have, we have not received in equal shares. A generous use of what we have, not a selfish accumulation of possessions, is what God asks of us. Reflecting regularly on God's lavish gifts to us may help us be more willing to share these gifts with others; whether they be the world's poor or my closest family and friends who need something that I have.

In gratitude for all you have given me, O God, help me each day to make my life a gift for others.

Friday: Luke 8:8
And some seed fell into rich soil and grew and produced its crop a hundredfold.

In the Parable of the Sower, Jesus was talking about how the word can be planted in people who listen and respond, bearing much fruit. He takes his example from the simplest of farming truths – plant a seed in the right soil and it multiplies. Our world is so rich in resources, and we can steward God's creation to produce so much more. There is more than enough for everyone. How tragic that we work the land for the benefit of the few, and where we have great excess of produce, people still go hungry.

Father, guide the nations and their citizens to work for – and demand – the basic rights for all – the food to live, the right to life and peaceful coexistence.

Saturday: Matthew 25:20-21

The man who had received the five talents came forward bringing five more. "Sir," he said "you entrusted me with five talents; here are five more that I have made". His master said to him, "Well done, good and faithful servant; you have shown you can be faithful in small things, I will trust you with greater; come and join in your master's happiness."

Whether we apply this parable to the particular abilities that we have as individuals, or to the way we use our world, the message is the same. Good things are to be cultivated so that we may not only be responsible for what we have, but so that others may benefit, too. Wherever there are hungry people in our world, wherever people lack basic necessities, we show that we are not using the world's resources properly. There are strong voices that speak out against such injustices. How can I add my voice to theirs?

Father, I pray for the world and its one family of people. May your gifts to us be generously shared so that no-one is ignored or turned away in their need.

Week Three
Loving the Feminine and the Masculine

Male and female we have been created. In God's image we have been created, but how do we relate with one another? The Spirit is calling us to more mature relationships of mutuality and respect. Both the masculine and the feminine have unique gifts, gifts that are of equal worth. Now is a good time to renew our attitudes and values towards both, to develop right relationships between men and women, thereby working to end discrimination and bring about equality in our world.

Sunday: Genesis 1:27
(31st Sunday of the Year)

**God created man in the image of himself,
in the image of God he created him,
male and female he created them.**

Week Three

From the story of Creation itself, God has shown that both male and female are an essential complement to each other and vital for the on-going celebration of creation. Politics and social attitudes have often blurred the distinction and we have confused the uniqueness of gender with the equality of individuals. In the eyes of God, the Creator, each one of us is uniquely held in existence by His love. I am valued as I am – male or female.

Father, in times when I am disappointed about who I am, and lack self-esteem and self-confidence, may I remember that you call me into being and you love me just as I am.

Monday: Ephesians 4:31-32

Never have grudges against others, or lose your temper, or raise your voice to anybody, or call each other names, or allow any sort of spitefulness. Be friends with one another, and kind, forgiving each other as readily as God forgave you in Christ.

This simple command is to all of us, women and men, sisters and brothers in Christ. It is a call to mutual respect and care. It provides us with a recipe for respect and friendship that overcomes differences and celebrates all that true respect may achieve in building up communities. True friends are neither subservient nor controlling. A good friendship recognises the gifts and the love that my friends offer me, and challenges me to give of myself to them.

Father, may your Spirit help me to deepen friendship and to respect the dignity of everyone I meet.

Tuesday: Colossians 2:6-7
(All Saints)

You must live your whole life according to the Christ you have received – Jesus the Lord; you must be rooted in him and built on him and held firm by the faith you have been taught, and full of thanksgiving.

Today can be a celebration for all those who are simply and sincerely trying to live their faith, often in very difficult circumstances, and probably with many shortcomings and failings along the way. Paul tells us that we are all called to be 'saints'; people who seek holiness in their lives, and remain alert for the opportunities that God may give them every day to bring His love to others. There are many saints whose lives of witness and faith are recorded in the history of our Church, but there are many others who are the silent witnesses, perhaps known only to God.

Father, look not on our sins but on the faith of your Church and grant us the peace and unity of your kingdom.

Wednesday: John 11:25-26

(Commemoration of all the Faithful Departed)

I am the Resurrection. If anyone believes in me, even though he dies he will live, and whoever lives and believes in me will never die. Do you believe this?

Today is the opportunity to remember those who have died and are still important to us. It is essential to take the time to call to mind those who have had an impact on our lives and helped us to become who we now are. We can commend them to God with thanksgiving. We should pray, too, for those who otherwise would be forgotten, those who have no-one else to pray for them – for that is the meaning of the Church as 'the communion of saints'. In our remembering, we should recognise the differing roles of both men and women who have had an impact on our lives.

Father, I give thanks for all those people who brought your love into my life. May they be blessed and rewarded for all that they did in your name. Hold all the departed in your loving embrace, and bring us all to new life.

Thursday: Ephesians 5:25,28

Husbands should love their wives just as Christ loved the Church and sacrificed himself for her. In the same way, husbands must love their wives as they love their own bodies.

Paul is sometimes criticised for his attitude to women. But in the context of his own time Paul was actually a radical thinker. At a time when women were regarded as property rather than as people, Paul encourages a sense of love and equality in marriage; a union of persons. Where are my prejudices? Do I believe there are things that men should or should not do, things that are only woman's work? These generalisations are gradually being eroded but am I making progress towards valuing the person for who they are and what they are trying to be?

Father, may I learn to see each person as made in your image, to be loved for who they are.

Friday: Mark 16:1
(St Charles Borromeo)

When the Sabbath was over, Mary of Magdala, Mary the mother of James, and Salome, bought spices with which to go and anoint him. And very early in the morning on the first day of the week they went to the tomb, just as the sun was rising.

It is often declared that Jesus chose only men to be His disciples. But He most certainly had women among His followers who provided for the whole group. It is also true that, particularly in the Gospel of Mark, Jesus moved His ministry forward by His actions towards women: the first pagan to be cured, the first to see the Resurrection, the only one to initiate her own cure, the one who stood at the foot of the cross were all women. One of the most important moments of Jesus' self-revelation was to the Samaritan woman in the Gospel of John. Men may have been disciples, but the women were so often the catalysts for his ministry.

Father, Your Son chose both men and women to be part of his ministry. May we share equally, as men and women, in continuing His ministry and building your Kingdom in our world.

Saturday: Luke 1:46-47

And Mary said: "My soul proclaims the greatness of the Lord and my spirit exults in God my saviour."

Week Three

Mary remains a model for our life in Christ and there is much that we can learn from even the few words she spoke in the Gospels and in the rare occasions that she is mentioned. She remains faithful despite all the misgivings and hesitations that must have followed her initial consent to do God's will. She endured all a mother's suffering at the betrayal and death of her Son and, after her Son, she ranks first among all people. She is the model for all, both men and women.

Holy Mary, Mother of God, pray for us sinners, now and at the hour of our death. Amen.

Week Four
Interracial Harmony

Many of us carry prejudice within ourselves, and we are all deeply affected by racism. As Christians, we are called to respect the gifts of all people. It is time for us to look honestly at the conscious and unconscious prejudices that we harbour so that, together, we can launch effective efforts to recognise and overcome prejudice and racism.

Sunday: Acts 2:5
(32nd Sunday of the Year)

Now there were devout people living in Jerusalem from every nation under heaven, and at this sound they all assembled, each one bewildered to hear these men speaking his own language. They were amazed and astonished.

At the first Pentecost, not only was the Spirit given to the Church but the invitation was given to people of every nation to listen. In the same way, the disciples had been commissioned by Jesus to "go out to the whole world, proclaim the good news and baptise". If I am to be an ambassador for Christ then I, too, must reject no-one nor exclude them. Our Diocese is the home for people from every nation, and it is here in my parish that I must build harmony and acknowledge the dignity of every person.

Father, may I see your Son in every person that I meet, valuing their gifts and meeting their needs.

Monday: John 4:8-9

The Samaritan woman said to him, "What? You are a Jew and you ask me, a Samaritan, for a drink?" – Jews, in fact, do not associate with Samaritans.

The policies of governments mean that many nations still live in conflict with one another and regard one another with suspicion. Although by history and tradition the Jews and Samaritans had no dealings with one another, Jesus broke through the barriers to speak with the Samaritan woman and offered her, and the Samaritans who gathered with her, all the benefits of His ministry. Can I be as free of prejudice and suspicion when I meet with people of other nationalities?

Father, give me true freedom to love you in everyone you place in my life. May those you bring to me find respect and welcome.

Tuesday: Romans 15:7.13

It can only be to God's glory, then, for you to treat each other in the same friendly way as Christ treated you. May the God of hope bring you such joy and peace in your faith that the power of the Holy Spirit will remove all bounds to hope.

Week Four

So often, we hesitate to make people who are racially different from ourselves feel genuinely welcome in 'our' towns or suburbs, schools, places of worship, workplaces or social situations. Jesus scandalised His contemporaries, however, by welcoming all people, no matter what their cultural heritage or social standing, into His community. Am I still stuck behind a wall of prejudice or just even unfamiliarity? What might I do to make that first step of welcome?

Jesus, you always welcome me into your presence, even when (particularly when) I am in need or things are going wrong in my life. Help me to be a welcoming presence wherever I go and with those with whom I associate.

Wednesday: Ephesians 2:20-22
(Dedication of the Lateran Basilica)

You are part of a building that has the apostles and prophets for its foundations, and Christ Jesus himself for its main cornerstone. As every structure is aligned on him, all grow into one holy temple in the Lord; and you too, in him, are being built into a house where God lives, in the Spirit.

The great churches and basilicas are important signs of the presence of faith but the real witness to Christ is not in buildings, but in people. I am asked to make Christ present, to be united with others in witnessing to Christ – just as tightly bonded together as the bricks and stones that make the building. There is plenty of room for diversity; just as building components vary in size, length and type of materials. To be part of the building, which is the Body of Christ, I must have purpose and take responsibility in using the gifts and talents that I have.

Father, may I be a part of the Body of Christ your Son by using my gifts in a ministry in the Church, by prayer and by action in the community in which I live.

Thursday: 1 Corinthians 10:32-33
(St Leo the Great)

Never do anything offensive to anyone – to Jews or Greeks or to the Church of God; just as I try to be helpful to everyone at all times, not anxious for my own advantage but for the advantage of everybody else, so that they may be saved.

It is one thing to accommodate other people and their different ways of doing things. This may help them to feel welcome. Equally important, as Paul wisely says, is to avoid giving offence to others in the way I behave; in what I say. I wonder if I am gentle enough and sensitive with others? Do I ever stop to think that what I am about to say or do may offend people that I have just met or am only beginning to know?

Father, make me sensitive to people, to be aware of their vulnerability and their anxieties. May I never shut people out by my careless words or offensive language.

Friday: Ephesians 1:15-16
(St Martin of Tours)

That will explain why I, having once heard about your faith in the Lord Jesus, and the love that you show towards all the saints, have never failed to remember you in my prayers and to thank God for you.

Paul was well accustomed to racial divisions and tensions during his travels. As Apostle to the Gentiles it was his first concern to bring the good news about Jesus Christ to all people to whom he preached in Asia Minor and then on his way to Rome. For him, everyone was worthy to receive his message, no-one was to be excluded.

Father, grant me an openness to all people. May I be an instrument of your love and peace at all times, in every place.

Saturday: John 12:46
(St Josaphat)

I, the light, have come into the world, so that whoever believes in me need not stay in the dark any more.

Throughout His ministry, Jesus met with opposition. Often it came from Jewish groups who were threatened and challenged by His teaching, but He found opposition from Gentiles and pagans, too. He never sent them away. He could criticise and speak harshly about their hypocrisy and blindness to Him, but His message was for all – "I came to draw all people to myself". If our faith becomes something for a select few, or it shuts people out, then we have limited the ministry of Christ and compromised all that he set out to do. My faith is not mine to own, but a gift to be shared freely.

Lord Jesus, I thank you for the invitation to continue the ministry that you began. May I never compromise your call to all to hear the good news of the Father's love.

Week Five
God's Human Family

As human beings, we are called to be one human family, to work towards peace in the world. Now is the time to end wars among nations, to stop ethnic cleansing, to cease the activities of rich nations which exploit poorer nations. We all can live together in harmony, which is God's plan of creation.

Sunday: John 17:21
(33rd Sunday of the Year)

May they all be one.
Father, may they be one in us,
as you are in me and I am in you,
so that the world may believe it was you who
sent me

John is writing his Gospel for a divided and confused community. He is emphasising those things which are most important and at the heart of Jesus' prayer is the plea that all may be one. But how often do I stand apart and deliberately distance myself from others: those who look different, have alternative opinions and lifestyles, choose other priorities? Jesus does not pray that we may all be the same, but that each one works to live in harmony with those around them: many diverse and varied people living in unity.

Father, in the diversity of people in this world, may I learn to value the differences, delight in the variety and seek to find You in those around me today.

Monday: 1 Corinthians 12:12-13

Just as a human body, though it is made up of many parts, is a single unit because all these parts, though many, make one body, so it is with Christ. In the one Spirit we were all baptised, Jews as well as Greeks, slaves as well as citizens, and one Spirit was given to us all to drink.

It is part of God's plan that we should all be different. He loves each one of us as uniquely created by Him. The brilliance of God's plan is that we should all be different, but all belong together. With our different gifts and abilities and needs we depend on each other and our world yearns for the moment that we work together as one. Friends do not need to be alike – quite the contrary. Our world will be in harmony when we each place ourselves and our gifts in service of one another.

Father, may we be the threads of colour which make up the rich tapestry that you have created so that, blending together, we may complete the image and presence of your Son in our world.

Tuesday: 1 Corinthians 12:4-6

There is a variety of gifts but always the same Spirit; there are all sorts of service to be done, but always to the same Lord; working in all sorts of different ways in different people, it is the same God who is working in all of them.

Without even needing to change my routine of life today, I shall see people in all types of jobs and activities, all caught up in their own responsibilities: men and women in trades and services, parents with children, children in schools and colleges; business men and women, civil servants and local government employees, the elderly. Everyone has their part in trying to make our cities and countryside efficient and safe places to be. God's Spirit is at work in them all. Am I working with a sense of working with others? Or am I just doing a job for myself, on my own?

Father, watch over the complexity of our lives and guide us all in making a difference for the good in all that we do – working in harmony with those around us.

Wednesday: Acts 10:34-35
(St Edmund of Abingdon)

Then Peter addressed them: "The truth I have now come to realise" he said "is that God does not have favourites, but that anybody of any nationality who fears God and does what is right is acceptable to him".

That was quite a statement for Peter to make, given his Jewish background and the heritage of being a member of God's chosen people. In our global world we have a new opportunity to discover the dignity of every person, looking past the divisions of race, colour and creed. But how ready am I to acknowledge the goodness in those around me? Do I look down on people because they are from the 'Third World' or because they do not speak my language?

Father, today I will seek to see the goodness in those I meet and to acknowledge that everyone has dignity simply because you love them.

Thursday: Mark 9:33-35

(St Elizabeth of Hungary, St Hilda,
St Hugh of Lincoln)

They came to Capernaum, and when he was in the house he asked them, "What were you arguing about on the road?" They said nothing because they had been arguing which of them was the greatest. So he sat down, called the Twelve to him and said, "If anyone wants to be first, he must make himself last of all and servant of all".

Jesus had just told His disciples, for the second time, that He would be put to death but would rise from the dead. But the disciples had not been listening and they were caught up in things that they thought were important to them – who was the greatest among them? Their question was not important but it was taking up their time and energy. Will I recognise today the time I spend on things that are of little importance, things about me and my opinions, things that have no value in themselves?

Father, my day belongs to you but I need your help in staying focussed on what is really important. Help me to see the distractions for what they are, and put them aside.

Friday: Ephesians 2:13-14

But now in Christ Jesus, you that used to be so far apart from us have been brought very close, by the blood of Christ. For he is the peace between us, and has made the two into one and broken down the barrier which used to keep them apart.

Central to the teaching of Jesus is the desire for unity and peace. There is no need for uniformity, Jesus rejoices in the diversity of people. Paul faces the constant suspicion of difference as he goes on his journeys preaching the Good News to the Gentiles. Centred on Christ, we are to live in peace with one another. In today's world, do I promote peaceful co-existence by the way I live, by my tolerance of diversity, my accommodation of the unfamiliar? Or do I make other people feel uneasy and self-conscious because I make them feel 'different'?

Father, make me a channel of your peace and a bridge of understanding between people.

Saturday: 2 Corinthians 5:20

So we are ambassadors for Christ; it is as though God were appealing through us, and the appeal that we make in Christ's name is: be reconciled to God.

We cannot just hope for peace and justice, or think it enough to believe in Christ. We are invited to be ambassadors for Christ. An ambassador represents, stands in the place of, acts for someone or something and does so with authority. Would people think that I am Christ by the way I behave, what I say, or by what they receive from me? Where should I place a priority for change in my life, so that this journey 'into the image of Christ' may take the next step forward?

Father, only by the help of your grace can I hope to be a fitting ambassador for your Son. May the power of your Spirit flow through my thoughts and actions today and always.

Week Six
The Trinity and World Community

As Christians, we are called to be a people of hope. Through the Church, the divine persons of the Blessed Trinity call us to renew the face of the earth so that the reign of God may be established.

Sunday: Ezekiel 34:11-13
(Christ the King)

'I am going to look after my flock myself and keep all of it in view. As a shepherd keeps all his flock in view when he stands up in the middle of his scattered sheep, so shall I keep my sheep in view. I shall rescue them from wherever they have been scattered during the mist and darkness. I shall bring them out of the countries where they are; I shall gather them together from foreign countries and bring them back to their own land.'

Kingship is not a particularly common or popular theme in the 21st Century but Christ's kingship is quite unlike any other. His kingship is underpinned, primarily, with compassion and protection for those in his care. Trusting in Christ does not make me perfect, or take all my problems away but it does give me hope and a sense of purpose and values by which to live my life. In this final week of Season V, I will keep in mind some of the reassurances that will strengthen my faith for the future and they can be a constant encouragement when I bring them to mind.

Father, may my journey in faith always be strengthened and reassured by your understanding of who I am, of my struggles to do what is right, and of your ever-faithful love and mercy.

Monday: Romans 8:26-27
(Presentation of the Blessed Virgin Mary)

The Spirit too comes to help us in our weakness. For when we cannot choose words in order to pray properly, the Spirit himself expresses our plea in a way that could never be put into words, and God who knows everything in our hearts knows perfectly well what he means....

Maintaining that sense of the presence of God is not easy. Prayer, and the whole question of communicating with God, is a mystery and, for most, full of distractions. But even our intention to pray is heard, and the task is taken out of our hands when we feel that we cannot pray as we would wish. All we need to maintain is the sense of 'wanting' to pray, and 'trying' to stay close to God in all things.

Father, for your gift of prayer within me, by the gift and presence of your Spirit, I thank you.

Tuesday: Matthew 28:20
(St Cecilia)
"And know that I am with you always; yes, to the end of time."

I am never alone. Christ remains with me. He will use others to be instruments by which He can love me. He will be present to me in the Eucharist – always ready to forgive me in the Sacrament of Reconciliation when things go wrong. But He is present to me always through the abiding presence of His Spirit, even though I may not be aware of Him.

Lord, in moments of loneliness and confusion, give me the peace of knowing that you are with me; a friend at my side.

Wednesday: Mark 6:6-7,12

He made a tour round the villages, teaching. Then he summoned the Twelve and began to send them out in pairs giving them authority over the unclean spirits. So they set off to preach repentance; and they cast out many devils, and anointed many sick people with oil and cured them.

In Mark's Gospel, the Twelve are sent out to do the work of Jesus and they succeed. The remarkable thing is that they manage to achieve great things even though they understand so little of what Jesus is teaching them at the time He sends them out. Even after their return we see in that Gospel that they still do not know what Christ is doing, or understand the meaning of His teaching or His miracles. Jesus had not waited for His disciples to be sufficiently well 'qualified' before He sent them out. He used them to achieve great things even though they were still beginners.

Lord, give me confidence to do your work, and to live my faith even while I may think that I know so little and feel I am unable, unfit to complete the tasks that you may set before me.

Thursday: Mark 4:33-34
(SS Andrew Dung-Lac & Companions)

Using many parables like these, he spoke the word to them, so far as they were capable of understanding it. He would not speak to them except in parables, but he explained everything to his disciples when they were alone.

It seems that the disciples were not even keeping up with the crowds in their understanding of what Jesus was saying. But this did not disqualify them. Jesus did not send them away simply because they were not His best students and quick to learn. He remains utterly faithful. He continues to be patient and encouraging.

Lord, even when I am slow to understand and change, may I always feel your encouragement and your invitation to begin again and to learn from my mistakes. I thank you for your endless patience with me.

Friday: Romans 8:35

Nothing therefore can come between us and the love of Christ, even if we are troubled or worried, or being persecuted, or lacking food or clothes, or being threatened or even attacked.

Sometimes – often – I can find that I have lost sight of the presence of God. I just get too busy, problems overwhelm me. I look for common sense and logical solutions and forget to ask for help and guidance of the Spirit. Fortunately, no matter how I might seem to distance myself from God, there is never a moment when He has allowed me to separate myself from His love – He is always there – always will be!

Lord, I thank you for holding on to me, as a mother holds her child. May your firm grasp guide me, pulling me safely away from all danger, and leading me in your way.

Saturday: Ephesians 3:20-21

Glory be to him whose power, working in us, can do infinitely more than we can ask or imagine; glory be to him from generation to generation in the Church and in Christ Jesus for ever and ever. Amen.

I do not have the whole vision of what God is about; it is mystery. I may not feel His presence and I may have no knowledge of what He is achieving in my life. The extraordinary thing is that He is always at work, using me as an instrument of His grace and achieving great things through me – although I may be completely unaware of it. Just sometimes I may glimpse what he has done through me when someone thanks me for something I did not even realise I had done for them. I can be sure that wherever, whenever He wants to use me – He will.

Father, despite my clumsiness and shortcomings, I thank you that you will use me in some way today to bring your Son to others. May I prove worthy of your trust in me.

The End of the Season

Final Meditation: John 20:8
He saw and he believed.

The prayerful reflection on the Scriptures is a gift and a tool which can help us in our faith and our understanding. On the day of the Resurrection, Peter and another disciple ran to the tomb because Mary of Magdala had reported that the tomb was empty. Peter does not understand yet what has happened, but we are told that the other disciple (thought to be John) went into the tomb. 'He saw and He believed'. The Gospel does not say that he understood, that everything about the Resurrection was clear to him. The disciple knew that he was witnessing something extraordinary, that he was touching something of the power and mystery of God and it was enough for him to step out in faith. Much of God's presence in my life will not be measurable, understandable or logical. But can I step out in faith on the next stage of my journey?

Father, keep me close to you and provide me with just enough to nourish my often weak and faltering faith. Help me to recognise my gifts and place them at the service of your Church, in my Diocese and parish. Be my companion and guide on my journey, and bring me home to you. Amen.

We hope you have enjoyed praying with this
Daily Meditation Book for Season V of *At Your Word, Lord*.

There will be resources for
daily meditation for Lent 2006

Please look on the *At Your Word, Lord* website for these resources
www.aywl.org.uk

Do look out for them!

Taking the next step…

Using the Daily Meditation Book is not the only way
in which you can take part in the ongoing renewal of the Diocese.

Have you considered joining a Small Community?
(you might know them as 'small group' or 'faith-sharing group')

These Small Communities are groups of about ten people who
meet together to pray and to share their experiences of faith and
life with each other. These communities will be a continued part
of parish life in our Diocese.

Look out for the opportunity to join one in Lent 2006!

*Check the At Your Word, Lord website to see which parishes have
small communities meeting.*

The *At Your Word, Lord* website
www.aywl.org.uk
will be in operation well into 2006. It will offer information of resources for faith-sharing and nurturing communities into the future.

PRAYERTIME *Cycle B & Cycle C*
A Faith-Sharing book, for every group,
for every Sunday of the Year.
For both Small Christian Communities and other church groups.
£6.99 each – trade discount available for 5 copies or more

Available from the contact details below

***For further information about renewal in
the Diocese of Westminster contact:***

Diocese of Westminster
Archbishop's House
Ambrosden Avenue
London
SW1P 1QJ

Tel: 020 7798 9000
Fax: 020 7798 9077
Email: aywl@rcdow.org.uk
Web: www.aywl.org.uk
www.rcdow.org.uk

Our partner in *At Your Word, Lord* is

RENEW International

If you are in a Diocese other than Westminster and you are thinking about a renewal programme you may like to contact them:

RENEW International
1232 George Street
Plainfield, NJ
USA 07062

Tel: 001 908 769 5400
Fax: 001 908 769 5660
Email: RENEW@renewintl.org
Web: www.renewintl.org
www.parishlife.com